# THE
# COURAGE
# TO
# JUMP

Extreme Career Change Success,
After Loss of Business,
Marriage and Hope

By D. Pennington

Library of Congress Cataloging-in- Publication Data
D. Pennington,
The Courage To Jump: Extreme Career Change Success, After Loss of Business, Marriage and Hope
Edited by: Maggie K.
Co-Edited by: London

Published by: Diverse Service Solutions, LLC, 4830 Wilson Rd., Ste. 300-1015, Humble, TX 77396
www.DwanaToldMe.com

For information about special discounts available for bulk purchases, sales promotions, and educational needs, contact Diverse Service Solutions Company Sales at VM: 1-832-308-0472 or info@dwanatoldme.com.

ISBN: 978-1-7366578-5-0 (eBook)
ISBN: 978-1-7366578-4-3 (paperback)
ISBN: 978-1-7366578-2-9 (hardback)

Printed in the United States of America

*Dedication*

*For my mother, Brenda, for always loving and supporting me. She has shared in all my joys, trials, failures, and achievements and helped shape and make me into the woman I am today. This book is affectionately dedicated.*

# TABLE OF CONTENTS

# INTRODUCTION
# READ THIS FIRST

T he devastation was too much to handle. I can truly relate to how someone could commit suicide; just end their life without a second thought. At some point I thought to myself, *So this is why people kill themselves.* The thought crossed my mind.

So here I am. I lost my entire business within five years. I wasn't sure what I would do next. Do I go back to the corporate workforce again after spending long and countless hours building up the business I once had? Or do I try to pick up the pieces of my financially ruined business and start over again? I came to my senses and eventually decided, *Nah!* And so I regrouped to being employable in the new workforce. It wasn't long afterward that I was able to land a decent-paying office gig through a temp agency, only to find myself in just six short months *back up a sh\*t creek without a paddle!* as the old saying goes. Is this currently your situation, or has it been your situation in the past?

Have you found yourself abruptly out of business or work? Have you been working for several companies, staffing agencies, or people and constantly finding yourself out of a job? Or being laid off time after time, doing a job you loved doing for so long, and you now often wonder, *God, why me?* Trust me, I know your pain.

In my case, I've experienced both situations! Just when I thought I was getting back on my feet, I was hit with another blow to my ego and self-worth. Another layoff, one after another it seemed. Now, granted, I was not too thrilled about my sudden change from once being self-employed to having to jump through employment hoops, hoping to land a permanent, well-paying job as I rebuilt and pieced my life back together. But sometimes the bad career moves and decisions we make come with a lot of uncertainties in maintaining and keeping a steady, well-paying job.

So there I was, unemployed and receiving unemployment checks for about eight months to a year. While continuing my own job search, I started to notice a trend. During various job interviews I went on for digital marketing, I was being told that I needed to have a four-year degree in business or marketing. *Oh, hell nah!* I thought to myself.

Has this happened to you? Getting all cleaned up and ready, putting on your best-fitted skirt, button-up blouse, and three-and-a-half-inch heels for this exciting, promising interview, only to be told during the interview that you will need to have a college degree or you need to have more years of experience for this position? Well, whatever the case may be, precious time has been wasted when that could have been disclosed at the beginning, before making a blank trip!

I'm sorry if you are anything like I was and in a situation like this; I couldn't go back to school for four years; I just didn't have the luxury of time. I had bills to pay, I had other financial obligations, and I was in a really tight bind! By this time, the thrill was gone. I needed a paycheck, and I needed a paycheck fast!

I know you are getting sick and tired of inconsistent paychecks, a capped salary, a low-paying job with limited income-earning potential, and job opportunities where moving up within a company is not allowed *or* only reserved for those "special types" of employees.

You need an extreme career change! Hell, I needed an extreme career change! That's when I began to hear more about working at chemical plants in the oil and gas sector. And how much money could be made working all the hours I wanted and getting paid every week. The potential of moving up into a prominent position was easy as obtaining a one-week course certificate! *Um,* I thought, *this sounds like the road to take!* Which at that point, I mentally prepared for a comeback!

I was preparing myself to be armed and ready, especially if I was planning to change careers into this industry. But even with all of the info I had obtained, I thought, *What if there's still no job, and how am I going to enter into this new industry with no experience?*

Sometimes we need to sit back, look at our circumstances, find ways to think outside the box, and develop ways to turn our situation around for the better. Sometimes, or should I say most times, the answer is staring us right in the face. It may be as simple as changing your surroundings or changing your horrific thoughts and mindset into something more uplifting and colorful. For me it was my mindset of finding and obtaining a skilled trade to be proud of that would ultimately lead me into a safety career with higher pay, and I knew just what I had to do to get there! You are more than welcome to follow me on this journey in what I like to call part of life's transformation.

In this book I will share with you everything you need to make the transition smooth and to be armed with all the proper knowledge. This is from my personal experience, as I've transitioned from a comfortable eight-to-five desk job wearing high heels to steel-toed boots, where work-life (meaning all work and somewhat of a normal life) is much more challenging, yet exciting and rewarding. As a result of the transition, I also earn a higher hourly wage. Therefore you can too!

The turn of events during my transition took me by surprise, and it was beyond breathtaking to have the pleasure of going to the White House twice! (I'll discuss that in more detail later in this book.) I just want you to understand that taking the leap of faith has completely changed my life for the better, thanks to my determination, faith in God, sowing seeds, and making that scary but necessary move to ultimately encounter the plethora of opportunities this industry can offer.

And I know you can achieve it too! There will always be some type of obstacle you will have to go through to reach the top of the mountain if you want it bad enough. In this book you will learn how to:

- Gain access to and utilize programs that pay you while learning a skilled trade

- Walk the walk and talk the talk in the plant industry

- Effectively network

- Determine how much earning potential you can make in each craft or office job

- Achieve your career goals faster

This book was written because, personally, I wish I had the same insight and guidance when I first started. This would have made my career change journey less fearful and much easier to navigate. But since I went through all of it the hard way, you can now learn from my past mistakes, experiences, and knowledge attained to get you there faster and easier than I did.

I hope this book serves you well. You can email me a few months into your newfound career to tell me about how well you are progressing and to share your success story. That would make my day! However, my backstory will come before some of the more detailed information. So grab you a cup of hot tea or coffee and keep reading. You are about to get the front-seat view on how my career change took shape and in ways unimaginable.

Now, let's get to it and make this dream into a reality!

# CHAPTER 1

# YOU WIN SOME AND YOU LOSE SOME

*Yesterday is not ours to recover,*
*but tomorrow is ours to win or lose.*
*—Lyndon B. Johnson*

First I'd like to tell you that all of the events that occurred in this book are true. It's a story that's unique to me and my situation. But some of the things I wrote in this book you may be able to relate to. Truth be told I was more like a spider caught in a web of unforeseen events. How was I going to make it out of my situation—both emotionally and financially?

I'm sure you know someone who's currently going through some type of dark cloud that inhibits them from moving forward in life due to personal or financial hardships, failed marriages, the death of a loved one, some form of abuse, and the list goes on. So much so that they can't see the forest for the trees.

This is a story like none other, so brace yourself. Where do I begin? My life was filled with dreams, hopes, and a series of events encountering both the highs and lows of just living life. I discuss having to face and tackle this demon I call self-sabotage as I overcame challenging obstacles every day. It's the story of my life; how I decided to take back, take over, and kill the beast; having to make that drastic career change and exactly how I did it, lived it, and felt it.

Now, let's see...It all started in early 1998 when I was working for several oil and gas companies as a full-time employee. I was a project administrative assistant supporting two engineers in the riser department. It was a comfortable, laid-back, posh, and safe job environment. I had my own cozy office with wall art, floor plants, a desk with a credenza and a hutch, and two midcentury accent chairs for visitors.

I also had access to the corporate gym, located on the first floor of the office building, to use whenever I felt the need to sweat off a few extra inches. I was scheduled to work nine-hour days with a one-hour lunch break, and that was plenty of time to run personal errands and whatnot. Back then I always had a job working for prominent engineering firms, and I always had the financial stability of a full-time job with good benefits.

But I was feeling empty. I wanted more from life and my work, and I realized that my income was capped because of my current position, title, and lack of a college education. There was no other position I could move upward into unless I had a degree to substantiate the move and the pay increase. I didn't like that. I wanted to earn more money and move up in the company doing something other than administrative in nature.

However, there were not many positions I could move into that didn't require a degree. I disliked the idea of only making a set amount of money, never being able to grow and make more money unless I were the CEO or the president of a company. I felt trapped like a hamster stuck in a hamster-wheel race, running around and around without getting anywhere. I wanted more from work life. I wanted some control over how much money I could make without someone else setting the salary cap for me due to my lack of a college education.

## Ask and You Shall Receive

Sometime in the year 2001, a family member (an uncle by marriage) presented me with the idea and opportunity of starting a minority woman-owned construction company. At first I was hesitant to even think about getting myself tangled up in such an idea. But as the discussion grew and a plan was somewhat laid out, the idea was becoming very appealing to me. It was like the universe had opened up and answered my prayers.

After discussing the idea with my—at the time—live-in boyfriend, he was on board, and it didn't take me long to decide that I wanted to do this. "Count me in," I said, with much enthusiasm and with great anticipation of our first business launch!

As I continued to work my eight-to-five, cozy desk job, I began saving a substantial amount of money from my biweekly paychecks to help start and finally launch the new minority woman-owned masonry construction business in the year 2001. I was then finally able to quit my safe, cushy job with the capped salary. But I was about to find out that it wasn't going to be that easy of a task to run my own business. At first it was really complex and challenging. We had to drum up new business and get the business fully certified with all the local government entities and transit authorities.

I had to sign up for and attend all the small business development workshops and networking opportunities for newly formed businesses. My uncle and I had to work extremely long hours seven days a week, and we had to quickly learn the ins and outs of working with and obtaining contracts from larger, more established general contractors. I also realized I was set to perform multiple roles as the CEO, network marketer, purchaser, and project manager, and he was the co-CEO, brick mason, supervisor, and estimator for the startup masonry construction company we launched.

Not long after opening for business, we were blessed to land our first couple of lucrative masonry projects. One was with the city of Houston, to help build a local community recreational facility for the elderly. It was a bid for new construction, a building built entirely out of glaze and glass CMU block.

Shortly afterward we landed a second project we bid on with a well-known local electricity service provider called Reliant. It was a bid for new construction to help build and install masonry cinder blocks ranging in sizes of four-inch, six-inch, eight-inch, and twelve-inch CMUs for their large-scale corporate substation service building, an over 10,000 square-foot facility.

## When Things Go South Real Fast

Things appeared to be going well—actually, going great! And then my uncle by marriage decided to switch gears on me during an agreed partnership. He stated that because he would do majority of the labor work, he should get more of the profits.

Now, mind you, the initial agreement between us was to manage and oversee multiple projects we bid on, including the management of subcontractors we hired to perform the work. The agreement we had was not for him to physically do the work! That would be a waste of our time, energy, resources, and effort collectively when we could simply bid and obtain more projects to manage. It seemed like a win-win to me.

But he was being greedy and defiant and wanted all the money in his pockets. He cared less about my sacrifice of quitting my full-time job to join him in his initial idea to start up a woman-owned construction company and my sacrifice of waiting over six months to earn a paycheck from our new startup business.

Truth be told he had no real liability. I sacrificed and agreed to have the entire business set up only in my name, per his recommendation! At first I wasn't fine with that idea, but now I know why he preferred it that way. Well, as the disagreement continued, he started not showing up to our first two awarded projects.

Then there were times when he did show up that he was being disruptive and defiant toward the workers. I saw that this wasn't going to end well. I had to make the decision to seek and hire some reputable subcontractors to start and help finish the projects that we were initially awarded.

My back and a\*\* were on the line, and I had no choice but to make boss moves! Especially since I didn't have bidding experience or hands-on masonry experience. But that all didn't matter; I managed to figure out a way to hire some of the best subcontractors to perform the work as well as supply all the necessary materials and equipment needed to do the job right.

That didn't sit too well with him. He was furious, needless to say, so he decided to try to start drama on the project sites. But because I'd already built such great rapport, business alliances, and friendships with the project managers and owners, I requested that he not be allowed back on-site, where he would be hindering the subcontractor's performance. So they happily obliged and kicked him off their project sites, and he was told to never come back again! I really did feel bad for having to do that to him, but what's a girl to do?

Of course, he was not going out without a fight. He threatened to sue me! Yes, you read that right, sue me! And he was the one creating tension, throwing tantrums, and being disruptive because I would not agree to change our initial business partnership arrangement to suit his personal and financial needs.

He wanted sixty percent of the net profits, while I was to retain only forty percent, because he said that I mainly performed the office clerical, project manager, and network marketing roles (you know…branding, scouting/networking, supervising, and marketing for new business opportunities). Yeah, the nerve. What a joke!

Long story short he did eventually sue me, and we ended up having to go to mediation instead of wasting taxpayer money with the shenanigans. My attorney and I could hear the mediator drilling and questioning my business partner in the room next door. The voices were getting increasingly loud, and the tone of the mediator was becoming more intense while he was trying to get the truth out my uncle. We couldn't help but to giggle at what we were able to hear in the neighboring room.

Nonetheless, it was all a serious matter to me, and I was not trying to pay him a dime for walking away and trying to sabotage the business! But at the end of all the turmoil, the mediator thanked me for having my stuff together to show him and prove that the business relationship was legit and the business transactions were current.

Unfortunately, the mediator had to give me the bad news. He said, "Because you two agreed to become business partners, he'll have to receive financial compensation once the projects are complete, and whatever profits were made, he shall receive fifty percent of the net profits."

As much as I hated to abide by the ruling, I ended up having to pay my former business partner a total of $45,000 once the project was complete and profits were finalized. Boy, was I pissed, but relieved that it was all over with so I could focus on continuing to build up my masonry business on my own and without disruption somehow.

## Deceit and Lessons Learned

Don't ever go into business with broke and deceitful friends or family members who have a history of unethical, bad business practices, and I'll just leave it at that!

Only two years into the business, I managed to run it well, and I made a pretty decent income since the business was booming around 2003. I became very good at networking, strategizing lucrative joint ventures, and connecting with various business owners and like-minded people from all walks of life, including prominent professional politicians.

I seemed to have always been able to resonate with people, no matter their personality and professional background. As the months went by, I became more confident in my business dealings, and I ended up marrying my live-in boyfriend.

Because of my innate ability and God-given gift, I was able to successfully connect with people who ultimately helped my business to grow, landing larger and more lucrative project deals. By this time, my husband and I were ready to move out of our small one-bedroom apartment to a more spacious five-bedroom custom-built home. The house was everything I'd always wanted and dreamed of.

In the year 2005, I joint ventured with other small, minority-owned businesses on a FEMA project. Our mission was to help rebuild homes and set up temporary shelter for those affected by Hurricane Rita, a category five hurricane that affected areas in Texas, Louisiana, Florida, Mississippi, and other areas from September 18 to September 26, 2005.

Even though the new joint partners and I made a significant amount of money from the unfortunate acts of Mother Nature, we were proud and honored to help thousands of victims who were affected by the storm. Meanwhile, my business was doing great, and everything was growing as planned. My marriage was strong and intact; I was doing very well for myself. I was on top!

## When Sh*t Begins to Hit the Fan

The year 2007 came along, and I noticed that the US economy as a whole was starting to tank. I was only five years into my business and found myself in a bidding war against larger and more notable construction companies. For them to stay afloat, they were bidding on the exact same projects that we smaller companies were going after.

And of course they won and we lost every single time. Because the new construction arena was so volatile, that forced small businesses like mine to tank fast. Before I knew it, I ended up losing it all and permanently closing the doors for good. That was a very awful and devastating time, indeed, for me.

In a matter of a few relatively short years, everything around me started to crumble. And I was suddenly looking at how my once-harmonious marriage and the lifestyle that I'd nurtured and built over the years slowly fell apart. In reality—and I really hate to say this—I was the main breadwinner of our household since I made the most between my husband and me at the time. I was now in debt. I had to find a plan B and I had to find it fast!

As I was sitting in my comfortable home office, staring out the arched window, watching the palm trees sway back and forth ever so gently, I was thinking to myself, *Is this my reality now? Is this my fate?*

Eventually, I resorted to learning everything I needed to know about internet marketing. You know the craze back then was "How to Make Money Online" or "How to Start an Online Business." I took several online courses and bought several e-books on the topic, and after the trial-and-error phase, I launched and started an online beauty supply business selling specialized hair products.

My first online venture turned out to be a hit and was successful over a course of two years being online! Within the first year, it generated over $97,000 gross sales. I believe my immediate online success was due to my relentless in-depth research where I saw a trend and a need for women who suffered from hair loss, whether medically or genetically.

It was a major comeback for me, and I was excited about the endless possibilities in that niche! But then I created other offline expenses that were not needed, and

I ended up paying a lot of unnecessary rental bills and two employee salaries. I quickly learned that as an online retail business, you must keep your costs to a minimum. But that is not what I did, so I ended up losing a lot of money in the end. I shut down my online shop, let go of two part-time employees, and moved out of my retail office space. I was really hoping to make the kind of money I was used to making from my former masonry construction business. There goes my plan B!

The bills kept piling up very fast, nonstop, and resulted in financial ruin! I then began to have marital issues. I felt like I wasn't getting the kind of support that one would expect to receive from a husband who I so desperately needed at the time. Whatever happened to our marital vows he had committed to? "To have and to hold from this day forward, for better, for worse, for richer, for poorer, in sickness and in health, to love and to cherish, till death us do part"?

Everything was coming at me all at once, it seemed. The utility bills past due, the mortgage in foreclosure, the car notes delinquent, the business loans now in the hands of debt collectors…It was so much pressure on me I could have just popped and dropped dead. I kept all this insurmountable pressure to myself. I felt all alone, drowning in a sea of debt. I couldn't depend on or go to my husband for financial help or mental support.

I will never forget those disheartening words he said to me. "Hey, you wanted to start a business, not me. You wanted to move into this big house; you knew I couldn't afford to help. That's your fault. You should have just stayed working at your job as an admin." It's funny he didn't say all of that during our destination travels, driving nice cars and eating at some of the finest restaurants, when he happily escorted me on several political luncheons and dinner parties. I dared him to say that to me as if it were all my fault and act as if he didn't care if we lost it all! As if all the sacrifices I made never existed.

I was married to him for over thirteen years and not seeing much effort on his part as a supportive husband during most of our lengthy marriage. Looking back on it, he was content smoking his herbs and other paraphernalia. He had no interest in doing better for himself financially or career wise.

He was content working at the bar earning tips because drug testing was not a requirement to do that type of work, I recall him once saying. It was that very moment I realized the impact of our ten-year age gap; him being nearly ten years older than me. I was young, ambitious, and hungry for what life had to offer me. And he was happy to ride my coattails for whatever life threw my way!

Other marital issues came into play over the years, like verbal abuse; words that came from the tongue that were so distasteful and soul crushing that it would pierce my heart like a knife until I felt it bleed out in pain. Then came the physical abuse. The last straw was when he punched me in the middle of my back while I was sitting at my home computer station. I couldn't tell you to this day what made him hit me with such power and rage in his eyes.

Maybe it was because I lost it all, and it was too much for him to deal with emotionally? He could have killed me with that punch, the male cop said as he was making a report. Yeah, it was becoming routine that cops were being called to our home for domestic disputes. I had had enough. Time to go!

I made the decision to file for divorce and I chalked it up to irreconcilable differences. I even gave up my two beloved West Highland Terriers to him because they would have had better living arrangements going forth, which would suit and accommodate their active lifestyle and love of squirrel chasing with frequent walks in the park. Considering the mental state I was in, I did what was best for them.

## The Walk of Shame

Deep down there was this hidden shame I felt for being a failure—a loser, a big letdown to my friends and family, to those who looked up to me. There was this self-disdain I had, feeling worthless and not feeling worthy of any man's love anymore. All these feelings came rushing over me all at once. These horrible emotions were tearing me to pieces; I was trying to be strong and hold it all in, but I just couldn't any longer.

Did you know that stress is a silent killer? Well, it can be. According to researchers at Yale School of Medicine, stress may actually lead to sudden death. Well, I felt it, and it nearly took me out! My life spiraled out of control. I lost a lot of weight; I experienced frequent vertigo and became unbalanced as if I were walking inside of a spinning ball, going round and round. My blood pressure was extremely low. I was stressing myself so much that it made me vulnerable to other potential health issues. To be honest I actually had no idea I was stressing out to the point of near death!

At some point I thought to myself, *So this is why people kill themselves.* Yes, it crossed my mind, but of course, I was too strong-willed to ever do that. Being at the lowest point of my life, where everything seemed to be ruined, including failed businesses, a failed marriage, debt and bad credit, no income, and the loss of my two beloved dogs, all I saw was the bottom of the dark abyss.

My mind began to form crazy thoughts. I clearly understood why people would consider and commit suicide in times of peril. But I'm telling you here and now, don't do it! There is so much to live for. I believe in God, and I had faith that He would help pull me through the valley of the shadow of death.

Eventually I had to face my reality. It was what it was. My house was up for foreclosure, and I had to sell my prized possessions, pack the things I planned to keep, and quickly move out. I had to finally say goodbye to everything that I once owned, loved, and cherished in that home, everything that I'd obtained and worked so hard for over the years. I had built my once-comfortable livelihood from the ground up, and now I had to give it up due to unfortunate economic failure and my refusal to let go of harmful situations and toxic people in my life.

After placing what I wanted to keep into storage, I moved back into my parents' home and I was declared homeless; I had no address to call my own anymore. When it was all said and done, ironically, a huge weight was lifted off my shoulders. I felt I could breathe freely again. I slept for what felt like a whole week or two, maybe even a whole entire month! I was extremely mentally and physically exhausted but relieved at the same time.

I fought the good fight. A new age and a new dawn were in front of me.

Let the renewal process begin.

# CHAPTER 2

# EXTREME CAREER CHANGE, SET IN MOTION

*If you fail to plan, you are planning to fail!*
*—Benjamin Franklin*

D espite my challenges and setbacks, my failed marriage, former dead-end career choice, and failed construction business were personal learning experiences for me. I went through the highs and lows, and because of those experiences, I am more resilient and confident enough to know that I can conquer anything I set my mind to. At this point, I wasn't afraid to take on any challenge that would come my way!

## Tip #1

This is the key ingredient to changing your circumstances for the better, to learn from your past mistakes, and to become more resilient because of it. If you want to change your job, your relationships, your career path, or anything else that stands in your way, all you need to have is a strong sense of who you are and the confidence to know that you can overcome any obstacle that presents itself. In life things are not going to always be easy—no matter how hard you try. Great opportunities and success come mixed with difficulties, shut doors, constant noes, and even some doubts among peers, but that doesn't mean you should allow naysayers and negative moments to paralyze you. Remember, the only way to fail is to give up. Never give up. You can do this!

## That Pivotal Moment

The initial thought of moving back in with my parents was a no-go for me. But with the reality I was faced with, I had no choice but to regroup. It was now time for me to seek employment again among the working-class community. I was faced with going back out into society. I sought out various temporary agencies to help me get reacclimated to the workforce, working the typical 8:00 a.m. to 5:00 p.m., Monday through Friday work schedule again.

Thanks to my past work history and experience, luckily, I landed a couple of interesting job assignments within a matter of weeks. One was at a local cable company, supporting their HR department on a short-term assignment processing in new tech trainees.

The other job was on a more permanent basis, as an email marketing specialist. Because I've always had a love affair with anything internet marketing related, I was thrilled about the job opportunity. I truly believe I was able to snag this job due to my extensive presentation style during my interview with the hiring manager of an international corrosion prevention company. I really enjoyed working in their marketing department. The position allowed me to be creative, utilizing my previous internet training and online business experience.

Everything appeared to be going well. But then, that dreaded moment raised its ugly head. You know, that moment when you find yourself on the chopping block. The big layoff. Well, it happened. I was the one who was let go from my position, due to a large budget cut in the marketing department, I was told.

Now I was back out in the job market, where I sought similar employment in the digital marketing field. I was constantly told I was not qualified for the job. It was usually for this reason or for that reason, but I knew what the issue was; either I did not have enough experience in the workplace or had no college degree handy. But I knew this stuff like the back of my hands. I ate, slept, and breathed internet marketing. I was a self-taught guru; I could even teach them a thing or two!

So I thought to myself, *What next?* This was becoming a merry-go-round, except this time the game wasn't fun for me at all. Sorry—but going back to school was out of the question at this stage of my life! And so the saga continues.

There I was once again, wondering how my financial outlook would turn out.

I found myself back in a state of limbo. I began to feel defeated and worthless all over again. I had also moved out of my parents' home into a new one-year lease apartment just so I could be within walking distance of the marketing job that I was laid off from. Feeling stuck and disgusted at my situation, I had absolutely no idea what I should do next.

I'm sure you've probably gone through something similar to, if not worse than, what I have? Or maybe you know of someone who is currently going through job displacement and is down on their luck right now? Maybe you're tight on money or lack available resources to kickstart a viable career change too? Don't worry. I know your pain, and I'm going to provide a solution to your problem!

Although I opted for a more extreme career change in order to knock down those steel doors I was facing, I will explain further in this book and provide all the details about how to make such an extreme change possible.

You will learn how I managed to turn it all around from being self-employed to finding myself back in a dead-end career path and then being able to turn things around doing the unthinkable: landing an exciting, promising career path in the oil and gas field. This was done, it seemed, in the blink of an eye and without any major out-of-pocket expenses.

What was really appealing about this type of career change was the fact that no college degree was necessary for me to quickly earn one of many high-earning potential jobs that the industry offers.

What is required of you is for you to simply follow along throughout this book, take notes, make the necessary steps and efforts, and you will see measurable results faster than you could have imagined. You will have the knowledge and confidence to transition and change your career path if your interest is to enter the oil and gas industry.

**My Disclaimer:** This is not a promise, but what I can promise is that you will not have or achieve results without putting forth any kind of effort on your part.

*But this I say, He which soweth sparingly shall reap also sparingly; and he which soweth bountifully shall reap also bountifully.*

*—2 Corinthians 9:6 - King James Version*

## To Do or Not to Do...Was That the Question?

I started getting questions like, "Why did you change careers to go into this dangerous industry?" and other comments like, "It's a man's world; it's no place for a woman. Aren't you scared?" Yep, these are the most common questions I get when I talk about where I work.

When I get these types of ridicules or long stares, it just makes me giggle on the inside. Questions and comments like these predominantly come from people who never had or faced challenges in life, those who are fearful of the unknown, or perhaps people who are content with earning mediocre wages and capped salaries. I hope you are not one of those people.

Besides, who in hell has time to be scared? Time waits for no one! I desperately needed and wanted to make this drastic change because of the many benefits this industry could offer. Are you at the point in your career and/or life where you've felt a strong desire to have a really exciting occupation that offers leadership, challenges, adventure, and promotional rewards, all while paying you top dollar?

Does working on construction projects only ten months out of the year and going on a family vacay the rest of the months appeal to you? Of course. It would appeal to many! Just think, the remaining two months you're off work could be used for extended vacation time to spend with family and friends until the next project starts. It's all up to you.

Does this sound like something you would be interested in? If so, you are probably asking yourself how to get started working in the oil and gas industry without any experience at all.

Here are a few things you should know:

- You don't need four years of schooling to work at a new-construction refinery plant in the oil and gas industry.

- In most cases, you can walk in a hiring office, submit your resume, and get hired on the spot as an inexperienced laborer.

- There's usually a short time frame for being promoted to a supervisory or management position after you've proven yourself through hard work and dedication at a project site.

- There are also numerous entry-level construction project office jobs that you can apply for that even pay you weekly.

- You can be NCCER trained and learn a skilled trade, all within seventeen weeks, and be put to work immediately, earning above minimum wage upon successful completion.

Another perk of working in this industry is being able to travel overseas and/or nationwide from project to project, all while getting paid a *per diem* upward of $150 per day, in addition to your regular hourly wages. (A *per diem* is an allowance for lodging—excluding taxes—meals, and incidental expenses. It's a daily allowance issuing a specific amount of money an organization gives an individual, often an employee, per day to cover living expenses when traveling for work. A *per diem* can include part or all of the expenses incurred.) The sky is the limit in this industry!

Believe it or not, there are people from different and even prominent professions who made the switch! People like professional retail managers, accountants, attorneys, executives from Fortune 500 companies, and many other types of professionals. They all gave up the comfort of their cushy and well-paid nine-to-five desk jobs to switch into this industry for the chance at further challenging themselves. Many do it for the adventure and excitement that this industry brings. And of course, the money too!

But wait a minute, don't think for one second that the switch you would make is going to be smooth sailing once you're in; it's not. There are many challenges ahead to meet and overcome. These things include the ability to grasp and learn new skills, different language barriers, the environment, and having to deal with oftentimes difficult, narcissistic people and personalities.

This isn't all fun and games. The dirty side of the oil and gas industry can be quite unpleasant to the sensitive, frail, and meek types. One thing is for certain, and that is you will either love it or hate it—there's no in between. Nonetheless, this industry and the work are way more exciting than your typical nine-to-five office desk job.

## CHAPTER 3

# THE MAKING OF A SETBACK INTO A COMEBACK

*The beginning is the most important part of the work.*

*—Plato*

## The Humble Beginnings; Let's Get Prepared

When you have a chance to start over or a new opportunity to make your life great again, you will invest everything you have on that last and only chance. Having that moment means more than you ever thought possible because sometimes there is not a second chance.

When you've hit rock bottom, you don't really care about having it easy the next time around, and the difficulty of getting to where you are trying to go doesn't intimidate you either. The only desire is fighting and clawing your way out the bottom of the barrel to get what you really want out of life.

I had that chance to start a new chapter, a new beginning in life, and in a completely new industry. I was going to fully take advantage of the opportunity presented to me. There was no going back; I felt like this was my final chance at achieving something greater for myself. It was a blessing in disguise and the beginning of a new, prosperous future. This was it—I felt this was the right move I needed to make for myself and myself alone.

I used all the money I had saved up before being furloughed to send myself to a two-week general industry, construction, and labor OSHA standards and procedures course that would introduce me to the oil and gas field, primarily the chemical plant industry. At the time, this course included:

- <u>OSHA 30</u>—This thirty-hour program is intended to provide a variety of training to people with some safety and supervisory responsibilities. Regulatory requirements will be addressed, along with hazard identification, avoidance, control, and prevention.

- <u>Hole Watch/Fire Watch</u>—Safety attendant training is designed to orient an individual with the site-specific requirements for acting as a safety attendant in the refinery industry.

- <u>SCBA/SABA Hands-On Training</u>—This will equip the learner with the skills required to safely inspect, maintain, and operate a self-contained breathing apparatus (SCBA). This training will be suitable for either confined-space workers or workers who may be required to use breathing apparatuses during fires or in hazardous environments.

- TWIC Card—With the Maritime Transportation Security Act, the US Congress mandated that workers carry an identification card. The TWIC card identifies the workers who have the authorization to access secure maritime vessel areas without an escort. A TWIC card opens more freight opportunities for drivers and those who want to work at a port facility.

- CPR/First Aid—This is specific to anyone needing or wanting CPR, AED, and first aid training. This course is recommended for safety professionals, teachers, foster parents, personal trainers, etc.

- HAZWOPER 40—This course is designed for students who are interested in responding to oil spills, hurricane cleanups, etc. HAZWOPER stands for Hazardous Waste Operations and Emergency Response.

- <u>Basic Orientation Plus (BOP) or Refresher</u>—This provides help to trainees taking the BOP. It provides an introduction to many of the safety principles that will be presented in that course. This also introduces numerous safety terms used in the course. Becoming familiar with these safety terms will promote a better understanding of the course material and the course exam.

## Tip #2

It is very important, in my opinion, to take some type of newbie or refresher training course for whatever industry you're planning to transition into. It is simply a better way to go! If you're trying to enter the oil and gas industry, however, training courses such as the ones I mentioned earlier can help you learn the various industry terms currently used, the lingo, and quickly get you familiarized with potential safety hazards as they pertain to OSHA.

Also, you should prepare to pass the necessary safety council tests to gain employment in this industry the very first time. (Refer to my industry study notes page for more information.)

Once you've successfully completed a similar course, you can expect to receive a certificate of completion and assistance with setting up at a local safety council's test site. I had to pass the Basic Plus before any company would consider hiring me.

The Basic Plus is a card issued with your training credentials imprinted on the back, which requires an annual update on any regulatory changes over the year. This card is generally a requirement to obtain and to carry for access to maintain work at a live refinery plant that is no longer under new construction.

*Figure 1: Dee, first entry job at the bottling plant, Fire/Hole Watch—Year 2014*

Most people in the class were there for the same reason I was: they were brand new and looking for an extreme career change into the oil and gas industry. Some had prior refinery plant experience and simply wanted to extend their knowledge, while others wanted to make their way into the safety professional side of the industry.

The training was fast-paced and tedious but very effective in preparing us to enter the refinery plant sector. As for me, taking these classes was essential for my career change to take place because I needed to know everything there was to know about this industry before going into it blindly.

Being ready and armed, I wanted this to open doors for me and I wanted to be employable immediately—so should you!

It wasn't long after completing the class and receiving my Basic Plus card that I landed my first gig in the year 2014 at a beer bottling plant. Although it was not an oil and gas refinery plant, I felt it was still a plant and a stepping stone in that direction.

Plus it would be the first job to add to my resume giving me some type of plant work experience. I was very excited to finally get a taste of what it would be like to work in a plant setting. The only caveat to this plant work was when I heard the not-so-good aspects of having to use the smelly and sometimes awful porta potty when it was time to go release and do the number one or number two!

Now, see, that part I was very leery of, meaning I would have to swallow my pride and adjust my mindset from using a normal restroom to now having to use a modern-day outhouse. I also knew that my work-related conditions and standards would be lowered quite a bit, but that didn't deter me from taking the leap of faith into a new and extreme career change!

Nonetheless, I was lucky to not have to experience the porta potty on this first project. They had normal, air-conditioned restrooms with stalls, located on the inside of the plant—whew, thank God! Anyway, I somehow knew taking this first bottling plant gig would open doors for more plant job opportunities.

It was a short-term assignment, but I was making a decent amount of money considering my lack of plant experience and the abnormally long hours I had to work, which were twelve hours a day for six days a week. My first gig paid me weekly at twenty-two dollars per hour, plus time and a half of overtime. You do the math!

Although my mind and body were not used to working twelve-hour shifts, getting paid twenty-two dollars per hour, plus time and a half, was very appealing to me. Before this I had worked the traditional office hours from 8:00 a.m. to 5:00 p.m., Monday through Friday, and was paid biweekly.

There was never a real opportunity to work more than forty hours a week until I changed career paths. Making the switch allowed me to save up a lot of money very quickly, but it all came with a cost. I was extremely exhausted from working these long hours. However, the money I made was worth it.

Many of us fear the unknown. It's natural; it's human nature. That's why getting past your fear and self-doubt gives you the confidence and courage to take the leap of faith with no regrets. When it comes to making a big change in your life like changing your career from something low-key and modest to something more extreme, you'll need to have the right mindset and, more importantly, have an end goal in mind.

Staying focused on your goal, having a positive mindset, and preparing yourself to the best of your abilities are the necessary steps to make such a big leap easier. Rushing into something new without being prepared is only going to make your experience dreadful. So make sure that you are prepared before making a career transition or any other important transition in life.

# CHAPTER 4

# GOING IN DEEPER: THE FIRST TRANSITION PHASE

*The most difficult thing is the decision to act,*
*the rest is merely tenacity.*

—*Amelia Earhart*

**P**eople are usually shocked, and some are impressed, when I tell them where I work. The type of job I perform is usually seen as dirty and wrong on many levels, but not in the way you think. Having worked at a new-construction fractionator plant, I know that these types of plants are typically bid on and performed by EPC engineering and construction companies. At this type of project site, there are no live, active chemicals running through the pipelines just yet, and that's something you would definitely appreciate.

Despite my choice when it comes to my profession, I am a girly girl. I still love wearing my high heels, makeup, and sundresses and curling my hair, but don't let that fool you. I feel at home in my coveralls and steel-toed boots as well. It's something humbling yet empowering to walk around these processing units that will handle hundreds of thousands of barrels of product every day.

You can learn the most amazing things there and form some of the strongest friendships and bonds with coworkers at the same time; it was and still is the case for me.

Remembering when I landed my first job in the industry as a hole and fire watch attendant for a popular beer bottling plant in late 2014, I was extremely excited and eager to learn all there was to know. The work was easy enough, and I was very confident that I could make it in this industry as a woman.

*Figure 2: Dee, a masonry finisher helper at a new construction PDH plant—year 2015*

Nonetheless, the next big job I landed in the year 2015 as a masonry finisher and helper really set the tone! Yep, that's me in this pic, all geared up inside of an over one-hundred-foot-tall steel refractory furnace/boiler tank, which was ready to be insulated from top to bottom.

It was very hot that day, ninety-eight-degree weather, and there I was, covered in a thin, white Tyvek suit, with a half face mask with filters around my neck and ready to be worn when needed. I was securely strapped up in a full-body harness, had cut-resistant gloves on, and wore what I felt at the time were heavy steel-toed boots. I was wearing all the necessary PPE (Personal Protection Equipment) to perform my task safely.

I had to work around a bunch of younger and older men who swore a lot, dipped snuff, and would spit it back inside an empty bottle...ewww! They made corny, sometimes funny, jokes most of the day. I was around unforeseen things that could fall from over twenty feet above, which could have badly injured, or worse, killed me. I also had to deal with extreme weather conditions, and that translated into being extremely careful about not getting drenched in rain or exposing myself to frostbite, hypothermia, or 105-degree heat exposure.

And you guessed it, I had to use the pink porta potty, but luckily they were only used by the women working in the field. I dreaded going into one for the first time, but to my surprise, it wasn't so bad! At least the women's porta potties weren't bad smelling and were kept immaculately cleaned, so that was a big plus.

Unfortunately I can't say the same about the men's porta potty. They would sometimes reek of a smell that was indescribable. Thank goodness I'm not a man having to endure that! For the record, the porta potties were cleaned frequently by a third-party outhouse cleaning company. Other than that I did not regret one single thing about my second new-construction plant job!

Just because you are a woman, that doesn't mean you won't do the dirty work or go through the hard stuff. When you get hired as a field hand and helper, you will go through and must pass the same physical tests as men. The guys I worked with expected me to get right into it and take care of some of the hard stuff as well. And they expected me to perform the work as safely as possible. I managed to challenge myself and do this second plant job without any major problems at all.

Working at a new-construction plant project is not all glitz and glamour. I was good with this though, because I got the additional site-specific safety training and I always wore the proper PPE for the task. This is essential for eliminating or minimizing any potential hazards and safety risks. But I quickly learned that if I wanted to adapt to this first-time new-construction processing plant gig, I had to be quick on my toes, toughen up, get my hands dirty, and talk the talk like the men and women who'd worked years in this industry.

So if you remember, at the beginning of the book, I mentioned that I had owned and operated a construction company before. That put me in a unique position where I had to interact and directly manage a lot of men on my subcontract projects. Well, that made me more comfortable with holding my own now in this macho cowboy plant life world. In general women make up only ten percent of the workforce in this industry, not counting the office positions. To be honest it is also harder for women to move up fast too. It's a male-dominated industry, and you have to expect that and do the best you can.

## The Good, the Bad, and the Downright Sinful

Now let's talk about respect and disrespect. Most men out here are really nice and helpful. But some don't like women on the job site, period, and they never will. They're just stuck in their old-fashioned ways. You just have to accept and try to overlook that. However, there is improvement with the younger generation's acceptance of women in the oil and gas workforce.

Nevertheless, you're sometimes working with over five hundred people every day, and that means you are going to encounter over five hundred different personalities. You're not going to like everyone, and not everyone is going to like you. You have to find and associate with people you like and those who like you back.

If you are not good with numbers, are afraid of heights, don't like to get dirty, or are afraid of long hours and hard work, then you should consider another career choice. You need to be a team player if you want to last long out here and have a respectable reputation. If you are impatient, no one can help you, and this is not the right job for you.

Working safely requires your full attention. I'm not trying to discourage anyone from pursuing this career. I just think it's important that everyone understands the ins and outs of this industry before getting involved in something that can possibly get them injured, or even worse, killed.

If you feel like this is for you, then I encourage you to give it your best shot and try it. As you can see, it is possible to make it in this industry as a woman. Arm yourself with a positive attitude, a good work ethic, and an end goal in mind that you want to pursue further, and you will have a successful career transformation.

The flip side to working at a refinery plant and/or construction site is that I found myself working with and around a lot of cheaters, unfortunately, both men and women. The infidelity rate may be higher than in other occupations. Some online studies and sources have shown that the trade industry is ranked the number one field for male infidelity. The ranking was as follows:

Trades:

- Infidelity rate for men: 29 percent

- Infidelity rate for women: 4 percent

Here's an excerpt: "People who work in trades seek extramarital affairs more than any other career industry. A whopping 29% of male cheaters are working as a plumber, electrician, or in a similar field. Interestingly, and only 4% of women users leading toward infidelity were in trade."[1]

Based off my perception and what I know for a fact to be true, the top reason it is possible for men and women to cheat in the trade industry is because of the irregular hours and the varied shift work, which make it much easier to fly under the radar.

The main point of my bringing this topic up is because I've met and known several women who either cheated on their spouses or just outright fornicated and laid on their backs, primarily with men in higher-level positions, hoping to get a promotion or step up from doing the tough field labor work to better working

---

[1]Lauren Hamer, "Study Reveals the Jobs Where People Are Most Likely to Cheat on Their Husband or Wife," *CheatSheet*, April 1, 2019, https://www.cheatsheet.com/money-career/study-reveals-jobs-people-likely-cheat-husband-wife.html.

conditions like landing an office desk or comfortable materials handler job. I will tell you right now, though, the majority of the time it never works out for those types. You'll more than likely find yourself on the chopping block and laid off sooner rather than later.

As a woman with morals and standards for myself, I have a strong disdain for adulterers and easy, promiscuous women who work in this industry. It makes it that much harder for women to be recognized who want to honestly move up in ranks through merit, hard work, ethics, and integrity.

So therefore, ladies, stay focused!

## Industry Expectations and Increasing Your Earning Power

Diving deeper into this chapter, we are going to talk about the industry expectations for working in a new-construction refinery plant. These are things that you need to be aware of if you want to work in the EPC oil and gas industry.

Some people do not have a college degree, myself included, but that shouldn't stop anybody from grinding hard and making it happen for themselves. This was my philosophy throughout life, and it helped me build a future and see no limitations.

Even if I ask myself at times, *What if I had one?* I learned that many types of well-paid jobs don't even require a college degree. You should not feel that you are at a disadvantage just because you don't have one. But don't get me wrong, I strongly advocate anyone to get a college education if you have the time, financial means, and/or scholarships to do so! Now, moving on...

There are several types of non-degreed, high-paying jobs offered to women (and men, of course) that you may consider working at an EPC oil and gas refinery. The average hourly pay rate includes but is not limited to the following positions:

- ✓ Fire Watch/Hole Watch/Bottle Watch—$17–$24/hr
- ✓ Laborer/Helper—$14–$20/hr
- ✓ Flagger—$14–$19/hr
- ✓ Warehouse/Materials Clerk—$14–$20/hr
- ✓ QA/QC—$19–$30/hr

- ✓ Pipefitter—$23–$34/hr

- ✓ Electrician—$24–$36/hr

- ✓ Boilermaker—$27–$40/hr

- ✓ Millwright—$23–$32/hr

- ✓ Crane Operator—$36–$55/hr

- ✓ Forklift/Cherry Picker Operator—$14–$18/hr

- ✓ Field Supervisor—$23–$38/hr

- ✓ Field Area General Foreman/General Foreman—$31–$46/hr

- ✓ Safety Tech/Inspector—$24–$42/hr

- ✓ Safety Documentation Specialist—$22–$34/hr

- ✓ Field Planner—$28–$38/hr

- ✓ Field Material Runner—$14–$18/hr

- ✓ Subcontract Coordinator—$26–$36/hr

If you start a full-time career in this industry, there are many opportunities to advance along the way. If you are willing to work hard and learn fast, you can move up quickly in salary and professionally. Let me give you an example.

An individual can start working as Pipefitter Helper 3 at eighteen dollars per hour, and with hard work and dedication, they can graduate to Pipefitter Helper 1 and earn top pay at twenty-four dollars per hour. And that's just being a helper to a pipefitter journeyman! If you become really interested in learning this craft, for instance, you can continue developing by being mentored, performing hands-on training, and taking a few core modules.

This will get you to a higher-pay journeyman level: Pipefitter 3 to Pipefitter 1, where you could earn up to thirty-four dollars per hour! There are other career pathways as well, for those who have the desire to pursue them.

## Tip #3

There are ten important qualities that are looked for in this industry:

1. The ability to learn fast

2. Working hard and for long hours

3. Enjoying working outdoors

4. Being a trustworthy team player

5. Being on time and dependable

6. Having leadership qualities and the ability to solve problems

7. Strong mechanical ability

8. Having a supportive and understanding family, as this job requires long hours

9. Being physically fit, especially if performing a skilled trade in the field

10. Being a self-starter

For those who are interested in working in this industry, there are a couple of things that you need to be aware of, however.

Yes, you will make good money. You can buy a nicer home, car, or wardrobe. The financial rewards are tempting. Yes, you will explore the world. You get to spend a lot of time at home between jobs, waiting for the next one. You will spend half your day on-site, and two to five hours commuting by car or bus.

You will share a seat with people who smell, snore, and fall asleep on you. You will see and hear things that you hope your kids will never have to. You will miss your family and loved ones a lot. Some relationships will be strained and some will end. You will dream and wish to be at home while working in horrible weather conditions. Yes, you will wonder at times why you do it and if it's all worth it.

Remember these things before taking this career path change. No, you will not get to attend every barbecue, party, wedding, birthday, or funeral. You will not be able to have lunch whenever you want. You will not be there all the time for your kid's birthdays. You will miss precious moments like your kid's first swim or their first bike ride.

You won't be able to call your family whenever you want. You won't be there to take your family to sporting games. You won't be there for parent/teacher conferences, school plays, or presentation nights. You won't be there to see your kids win medals. You might not be with your family in times of crisis.

The people who work in this industry are making crazy sacrifices to make their dreams come true. We have to give up time spent with our families to make sure that they have everything they need. I'm living proof that my recommendations work. The requirements are simple, but getting this job and doing it well requires a determined effort on your part. If you have the following attributes, it will be helpful:

- ✓ Good work ethic, as slackers can't exist in this environment

- ✓ A positive attitude and a strong mindset

- ✓ The ability to get along with people from different cultures and backgrounds while working in hostile or isolated environments

- ✓ A good sense of humor to get through tough situations

- ✓ A bit of luck can also help

## Crossing Over to the EPC Oil and Gas Industry—What to Be Aware Of

Just to recap, here are some key takeaways to remember when deciding to enter this side of the new-construction chemical plant industry.

### Safety

To ensure a safe working environment, there are plenty of standard practices and regulations. While on the job site, employees are required to wear PPE. There is a lot of gear that you need to wear for your safety, and it does require some personal magic to figure out how to put your hair up while wearing a hard hat, but you will figure it out, trust me. Always make sure safety is the number one priority when working in the plants. Anyone who starts a career in the oil and natural gas industry should make a habit of prioritizing safety above all!

### Drug Testing

When you work in a plant-refinery environment, complete lucidity from all workers is required to make sure that everyone is safe. That's why, in the oil and natural gas industry, drug testing during the hiring process and while employed is a standard routine that is practiced everywhere. Drug abuse is not tolerated in any way.

This practice makes sure that everyone working in the plant is safe, since recreational drugs have (besides other effects) the ability to impair our reactions or thinking. For someone who uses drugs, this job is not guaranteed because there is regular and randomized drug testing for all workers.

## Working Conditions

Working conditions may vary. This can include working in weather conditions consisting of all four seasons and being in very close proximity to moving vehicles, various motorized equipment, and loud noises from time to time. Be advised, however, this is not a place for people who are easily offended, timid, or intimidated. Those who choose to start a career in the plant refinery will either grow thick skin, or they will just leave altogether.

Another important note I feel is worth mentioning is that you will also work long hours, often several weeks in a row, without any time off. That's typically called "turn-around" shift work. What that means is that there's a deadline to take the plant to a shutdown state so that critical repairs can be performed. That's when long hours are needed to complete the repairs in a timely fashion, so the plant can go live again and into an operational state. Hours like these are usually short term, maybe around three to five months before the turn-around project ends.

Refinery plants under new construction would typically have shorter work hours, such as a fifty-hour work week and a Saturday, which would then be a sixty-hour work week. But typically, no more than that and off on Sundays for the most part. Also some new construction schedules only work fifty-hour work weeks and are off every weekend. But that solely depends on that specific project's site job requirements.

A live refinery, however, operates twenty-four seven, and manpower is required on-site all the time. Operations personnel will work half the time in the night shift. This working schedule will disrupt your sleep, and you will seem to never feel adjusted to it.

Even those who work daytime jobs might find themselves working the night shift in unusual situations.

This might be one of the most challenging things to do for most people who don't want to spend time apart from their families. However, the advantage in this type of circumstance is that there are a lot of opportunities to be paid overtime!

Granted, this industry is not for everyone. To work here, it is required to be the kind of person who doesn't mind getting their hands dirty, their boots muddy, and working in—most times—extreme weather conditions, all while being aware of the importance of safety.

## Job Hazards

Chemical refinery plants are full of hidden dangers if they are not respected. Safety awareness is a full-time job, and even with all of this, accidents can and do happen. In my short four years (at the time of writing this book), working for nine different project site plants, there have been several work-related incidents that I've either witnessed or heard of through weekly corporate incident reports.

But not to worry too much; your everyday risk of getting injured or hurt on the job is very low in this industry, compared with others. Statistically speaking this is not that much different from other workplaces. People who work in a processing plant are very safety-conscious, recognize the hazards beforehand, and are doing everything to mitigate them.

# CHAPTER 5

# THE BIG BREAK: THE SECOND TRANSITION PHASE

*It is wonderful what great strides can be made when there is a resolute purpose behind them.*

—*Winston Churchill*

L isten up! I want to tell you about a great program that I used as an opportunity to propel my extreme career change forward. It all started in the year 2015, when I was laid off after the completion of my second plant project. This time I was prepared, and I had a decent amount of money to last me until my next big job. I was also much more confident that I would land another job in the new-construction processing plant sector, especially with the knowledge I accumulated after performing insulation and paint coatings.

I soon realized that these skill sets were not very popular in the EPC oil and gas industry, so I had to find something else to get into. The money started to diminish really quickly, and I had to get back to work fast. I reapplied for unemployment, and I signed back up with my local Workforce Solutions to get help finding a job in the industry.

I recall working with a very friendly safety manager at my first real new-construction processing plant job, and I remember his suggestion of trying to get into safety. I started looking at what types of jobs I could do within the safety field without a college degree and without having to spend over six months in a training room to get a certificate to do so.

As I dove further into learning more about the potential job opportunities, safety increasingly piqued my interest. I would have the opportunity to learn all there was to know about working safely at a refinery plant, including helping others in the field, preventing potential accidents, injury, or even worse, death! Plus the pay would double what I was making as a paint and coating specialist at the time, and I also would play a very important role that would help keep workers safe and in a healthy working environment.

I started looking into various safety courses and training centers, and I found a school that would offer a specific certification I needed, which I could complete in a very short period. It was for those who already had prior plant refinery work experience. It was called the Construction Site Safety Technician Certification (CSST). I loved the idea!

I used the little money I had left in my bank account to sign up for this course online. After a very short waiting period, I started the class alongside fifteen other people who were looking to get their safety certification as well.

After getting to know my fellow classmates, I learned that no one else had guaranteed jobs waiting for them after passing the class—except for one or two students in the class, including myself! But I felt confident, nonetheless, that I would land a safety job in no time.

I passed the class with flying colors and earned my CSST, an NCCER certification, which made me feel invincible and more confident in the steps I was taking to reach my new career goal.

On the last day of training, I exchanged numbers with several young ladies from my class to keep in touch personally and to help each other look out for any viable job prospects that may come up.

## The Earn While You Learn Program and the Power of Networking

Around mid-November in the year 2015, and about a week or two after graduating the CSST course, one of my former classmates called me to let me know about a great opportunity offered by Workforce Solutions. A prominent EPC oil and gas company had created a pilot program that provided accelerated, accredited training for female pipefitters.

They were offering hands-on training and direct job opportunities for women and veterans who were interested in learning a skilled trade while being paid, which sounded amazing! (Refer to my industry study notes page for more information.)

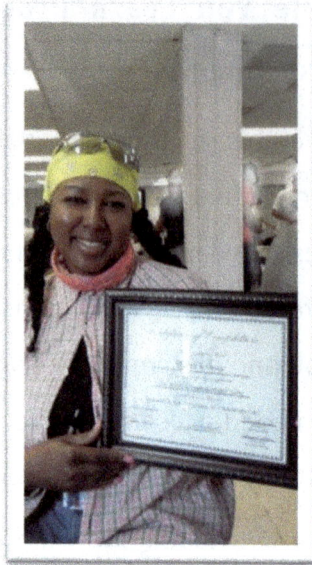

*Figure 3: Dee, a Pipefitter Helper 3, received program certificate—2016*

This was a great opportunity to advance in my safety career and open another door for future long-term employment. Actually this was the *exact* opportunity I was looking for, and I was going to get it from a company that prided itself on its outstanding safety record and having earned approval into the Voluntary Protection Program (VPP), OSHA's official recognition of the outstanding efforts of employers, and its employees who had achieved exemplary occupational safety and health!

The EPC oil and gas company I was interested in receiving skilled trade hands-on training from offered a program called the Women in Construction Program, which I am forever grateful for. They had collaborated with Workforce Solutions and other organizations. It was a seventeen-week course in pipefitting that allowed you to earn while you learned. I am thankful to God that I found out about this program as soon as I did.

I would have to go through their screening tools, which would identify candidates who would work well in a construction environment. It included a series of preliminary-grade school aptitude tests and initial interview questions. I would attend the company's forty-five-minute program presentation and then later follow up with a direct interview with the company. I later learned that among the four thousand women who initially applied, I made the cut down to the top twenty prospects. Wow! That was nothing but *God*!

Once I was accepted as a trainee into the skilled trades training program in January of 2016, and after completing and passing the seventeen-week course, I knew without a doubt that I had the proper skills, knowledge, and confidence to move forward. I was offered a permanent position as a full-time employee, receiving a Pipefitter Helper 3 starting hourly wage of sixteen dollars per hour, with all the overtime I could manage, including health care benefits. I was immediately put to work at one of their fractionator field projects.

I must admit that once out in the plant field, the job wasn't glamorous, but I worked my way up from Pipefitter Helper 3 to Pipefitter Helper 1 in a matter of two short years, which also increased my pay from sixteen dollars per hour to twenty-four dollars per hour.

I performed challenging pipe-fitting tasks such as grinding, beveling pipe spools, performing bolt-ups, and installing gaskets for high-pressure hydro testing of various-sized pipe spools and valves. More than ever I was working most of the time in extreme elements and having to deal with all kinds of wild critters and creepy crawlers too!

Now, just for giggles, please know that your girl—yep, that's me—was not feeling or having any of those damn creepy bugs and wild critters get on me or near me, not one bit! I would holler and scream so loud even at the thought of one inside my toolbox when reaching for a tool.

Unfortunately for me there were a lot of jokesters I worked around who loved to be entertained in that way.

But I persevered thanks to my never-wavering ambition. I was driven by not only having an end goal in mind but also the help and guidance of a couple of assigned mentors to help me further understand and hone in on my skills and the tasks at hand.

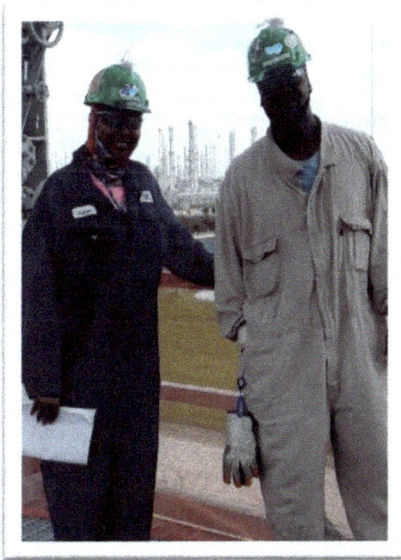

*Figure 4b: Dee, a Pipefitter Helper 2; and my former Pipefitter Journeyman/mentor; performing hydro testing at a frac project—2016–2018*

I had to work with two Pipefitter Journeyman mentors during my seventeen-week course who were chosen for me at the time. They were qualified and exceptionally skilled in their trade and was careful to not put me in harm's way from a safety standpoint. I am forever grateful for their show of support while I navigated the intimidating pipe maze world.

Although one of my mentors was a bit tougher on me, he claimed it was to help toughen me up while in the field...although I beg to differ!

After two years in the field and three years in safety, I can say that not only have I learned a skilled trade as a pipefitter helper but I have since received several quality raises, and a 5-Yrs of service gold and diamond pendant from the company, while working at several of the new-construction processing plants!

With that big leap in the direction I was initially aiming for, I was armed and ready for a purposeful future ahead of me. And with a pretty decent salary, it allowed me to fully support myself without much financial worry.

## Tip #4

Self-preparedness, perseverance, hard work, and having a goal in mind really pay off, especially when you have a clear end goal in mind. Without having an end goal that I had initially set for myself, which was to become a safety professional with financial stability, I probably would not have recognized or clearly seen the opportunities that were in front of me. More importantly, I would not have been able to get where I am today.

That's why I strongly encourage you to have an end goal in your mind, as well, before making life-changing decisions about which career path you want to go into for the long haul. Your goal in mind should work like a GPS to guide you closer to your destination. Once there you should be able to see the opportunities in front of you, which will clearly guide you further in that direction until the end is reached successfully. Having clear goals can bring clear results!

# CHAPTER 6

# MAKING BIG MOVES TO THE WHITE HOUSE

*Change doesn't come from Washington.*
*Change comes to Washington.*

—*Winston Churchill*

*Figure 5: Picture of the White House building and inside views.*
*From left to right: politician meeting room,*
*back of White House, stairwell hallway*

## Making Changes and Going to the White House...Round One

T he Women in Construction Program helped train me and got me into the EPC oil and gas industry as a permanent fixture. I am now working in the company's coveted safety department, as I said before. Although it was a great opportunity to earn while I learned a new skilled-trade profession, it gave me the best chance to generate a good income without having a college degree.

89

This is exactly the kind of opportunity that companies like the one I work for are offering to help more women and veterans like yourself, who need skilled-trade training, a job, and a career change in general.

On July 19, 2018, a former classmate and I, two of the remaining successful students of the program, were flown to the White House. We were sponsored by our employer to attend the signing of an executive order by President Trump called the Pledge to America's Workers. There were 430 other companies, trade associations, and unions that had signed the pledge as well, promising to provide education and training opportunities for American students and workers over the next five years.

Little did we know, after the signing of the executive order, that we'd be whisked away to the adjacent White House Lawn, where all the big-name news media was set up to do reporting. We were then told that we were invited to do a live news report on Fox Business with *Varney & Co.* Can you imagine the jitters and nervousness we both must have felt just learning this huge, scary request? Can you say, *Oh my God*?

## Lights, Camera, Action

*Figure 6: Dee at the White House Lawn, preparing for a live Fox Business interview—2018*

Five, four, three, two...

The camera was rolling. I was introduced first and was asked the first set of brief questions by Mr. Varney. We talked about the program and what it had to offer. We also had the opportunity to share with the news media about the company we work for and how they helped us tremendously as we got back on our feet by attending their training program.

Despite our anxiety, nervousness, that initial big lump in my throat, and the heart-dropping fear of messing up in front of the nation, we went live on the air and we nailed it! The airing of the show was titled "Opportunities for Women in the Trade Industry Are Growing." You can search and watch that video title directly on Fox News's YouTube channel if you care to watch it.

So technically that's how I got the first opportunity to go to the White House with my former classmate. Although we learned later that year, our role to help this movement was very important! We agreed to continue to tell our truths—our personal stories from how we ended up being jobless to where we are today with the company.

And we also explained to our local government officials, congressmen, and congresswomen why this program is important to us and for all the American workers in general. What I know to be true is that there are plenty of Americans who do not have the college education that is usually required to land a high-paying salary doing the job they love.

These same Americans, both women and men, aren't the typical college-bound types, but they still want and deserve the same fighting chance to work at well-paying jobs that will treat them fairly and earn them an honest wage as well as help them to create and live a comfortable lifestyle for themselves and/or their families.

Looking back on it now, I could not believe I was there on that mission. It was surreal. I remember feeling like Neil Armstrong; preparing to do something important for our future, our fellow Americans, and our country. In the following year, 2019, at our company's training facility, we had a surprise visit. It was Ivanka,

Trump's daughter! We finally met one-on-one with Ivanka, and I recall her as being very approachable, down-to-earth, welcoming, articulate, poised, and very professional.

If you've never met her in person, she is a tall, sleek, and slender, a very elegant and attractive woman with an inviting, warm smile and an infectious personality. She had a fun, playful side to her that caught many of us by surprise! Her playfulness with the former program students was much welcomed as it made everyone in the room that day feel at ease and relaxed due to her presence. It was a pleasurable experience to be around her. I can truly say she's a cool, laid-back chick!

During my continued support of getting the bill passed into law, along with the other colleagues of mine, I also had the pleasure to speak to several other prominent senators, congressmen, and congresswomen, sharing my story wherever I was guided to go.

## Second Time's the Charm—Back to the White House...Round Two!

It felt really good to have the honor to be invited back to the White House for the second time! The first trip was when the executive order was being introduced and signed by the president, and the second trip was a request for my presence to be there in support of a fellow student who attended the second round of the Women in Construction training program sponsored by our employer.

She was asked to give her brief story in front of the press and president, along with other American workers. Needless to say all she knew during the trip to the White House was to come prepared for a possible speaking part. She was scared and nervous as hell, but I assured her that she had this! When it was all said and done, she nailed her part and did an awesome job delivering her message!

During both trips to the White House, I stayed at the posh and elegant Trump International Hotel! It was one of the most beautiful, luxurious, and royalty-themed hotels I've ever had the pleasure to stay at. From the time

I stepped inside the hotel, my eyes uncontrollably jumped around, viewing various themes with delight, trying to grasp and take in all of its sparkle and beauty, starting from the very courteous and impeccably dressed concierge service from both men and women to the lavish bar and buffet of hors d'oeuvres located on the first-floor terrace. Even the timely room service delivery to include the setup of my private dinner table ensemble was something to behold! Everything was divine and presidential, just as I had expected.

Words cannot describe the stunning scenery there, so I included a few pictures for you to see for yourself. Although the pictures do not do it much justice, take my word for it, the hotel where I gladly and comfortably laid my head was one to be added to the notch on my belt.

*Figure 1: An inside look at the Trump International Hotel in Washington, DC—2018 and 2019*

I won't bore you with all the details of the White House trip, but I must say it felt like one of the most rewarding and uplifting accomplishments to help get an important bill passed for the good of the American people, especially women. I am so glad that I had a part in helping to change the future with expanding programs that educate, train, and reskill American workers from high-school age to near retirement.

This program helped me in a time of need, when I didn't know where to turn and what I would do for my future, and I am sure it will help plenty of other women; people in general as well. Having the ability to earn while you learn a skilled trade that is going to provide you with a generous income is a good thing that can save people from critical financial situations.

Some people are trapped in jobs they don't enjoy and are underpaid specifically because they cannot afford training. Sometimes the training can take a long time to complete, and they still must find a way to support themselves or a family during that period. I am hopeful that many people will find a program like the one I went through; it is a great opportunity to earn above-average income without a college degree. In July 2019, the bill was finally signed and passed and was made law. Our mission to help pass the bill had been a success!

The next photo you are about to see is from my initial visit to the White House. I was located at the South Lawn, near one of the entry points, posing after completing a Fox News interview segment along with a few other news media outlets that were stationed nearby.

*Figure 8: Dee at the White House—2018–2019*

# CHAPTER 7

# GETTING YOUR FOOT IN THE DOOR

*When you're committed to something,*
*you accept no excuses, only results.*

—Ken Blanchard

F inding a job in this industry requires a different approach for each company, as each one has its own methods and behind-the-scenes practices for hiring. Yet individuals who are looking to start or continue their careers in this industry need to know about the common ways to find a job working at a refinery plant.

## Company Websites

Before they advertise anywhere else, most companies will post open job positions on their official websites. Some companies use the website as the only place to post about particular job positions. Candidates can apply directly from these websites in most of these cases, and they can find all the details needed there as well.

If you are interested in getting hired by a specific company, it's best to regularly check their websites and see if they have any new job openings. (Refer to my industry study notes page for more information.)

## Job Portals and Career Websites

Another popular way to search for private company jobs online is by using career and/or career training websites like ShaleNET and Women's Energy Network or industry-specific sites like Rigzone.

You can also find websites that are general job portals like CareerBuilder or go to sites like Indeed, Jobs.com, or even LinkedIn, which is another good, viable source to use. You can create accounts on these websites and get notified when new job openings in this industry are available.

## Friend and Coworker Referrals

Another popular method for employers to get in contact with the workforce is by asking their current employees about who they recommend for open positions. These employees are people who have demonstrated knowledge in the industry and a good work ethic, and they can diminish the risks when hiring a new person.

Employers trust these individuals and rely on their good judgement of character because they see them as the type of workers their referrals must be! Employers know that no one will risk their reputation by recommending a person who is not committed to working seriously and giving their best.

Another great avenue for those who are interested in joining the oil and gas industry is to start asking friends and family about others who are working in this industry. Connecting with people who are currently employed in the industry can be a great way to get your foot in the door for future plant job opportunities. This type of referral method usually works about ninety-five percent of the time, so get to sourcing your close friends and relatives!

If you somehow got your foot in the door through a referral but need to ensure future employment and stay relevant for new and upcoming job opportunities, then networking with people in the industry can make a huge difference in the advancement of your career, so don't take this step lightly, and don't be afraid to network as much as you can!

So swallow your pride, get past your fear and anxiety of whatever could hold you back, and network, network, network!

## The Experience Factor

Many companies in this industry place a high priority on the experience of the candidates they hire. This can be difficult for young candidates who didn't have the opportunity to gather any on-the-job experience.

The amount of experience they require varies depending on the occupation. Nonetheless, there are entry-level positions that can be used as a stepping stone to take on this career path.

Internships or other learning opportunities while working can be used as leverage to get the experience needed for future employment. For those people who transition into this industry from other sectors like skilled trades, e.g., manufacturing, the experience they had working there can be used to showcase their related abilities, communication skills, work ethic, and leadership.

If you have no experience and want to find these entry-level jobs, here's what you have to do: try and get all the right certificates before applying to the specific plant jobs you want, and implement some creative online job-hunting strategies after that. And make sure your resume reflects your recent training certifications by listing them out one-by-one in bullet-point style.

If you have any forklift, construction, or supervisory experience that's not oil and gas related, that's okay. You can still use those skills and add that to your resume. This all can help you in the long run. Also you can find an entry-level job working on a service or oil rig, running a pressure or vac truck, delivering pumps and pipes, etc.

## What If These Jobs Aren't Posted Online? How Can I Find Them?

I just may have the answer for you, and the answer comes from me doing the hard work of trying it myself! Many don't know about this great opportunity to get into this industry without having any prior experience. It's something I already mentioned in previous chapters, the earn while you learn type of programs.

These programs are available for anyone who desires to learn a new skill and/or skilled trade with the promise of getting a full-time job with benefits after you pass all the testing modules inside the program. These types of programs usually take fifteen to seventeen weeks before you will be offered a job.

Companies like the one I work for and many other companies like them offer these programs as leverage for those who want to learn a skill or trade and change their careers without having to deal with the pressure of not being compensated while learning.

This is a great time to get your foot in the door pursuing this new career. I hope that through my book, many people will find out about this great opportunity and get to change their lives for the better. I may provide you a core list of companies that may offer some form of these types of programs. (Refer to my industry study notes page for more information.) Now how simple is that!

# CHAPTER 8

# THE IMPOR-TANCE OF NETWORK-ING AND INTERCON-NECTIONS

*You are an average of the five people you spend most of your time with.*

*—Jim Roh*

A s I leaped into a new career and a completely different industry altogether, I didn't know what to expect from the people who I was about to meet. Like any one of us, I thought that I would feel and be treated like an outsider, and I worried that I did not belong. I am glad I was wrong about all of that!

The people who I came across while entering this new industry were kind and warm-hearted, and I immediately started to connect to many of them. It was a very nice surprise to see that these were people just like me, who were trying to make it out of the rat race and survive. They were folk who were looking to make more money than the average and were willing to hustle hard. This was way more than I expected to see and learn.

I'm talking about hard-working people who aren't afraid to get down and dirty, who don't mind working long hours to complete a difficult task, but most importantly, who understand that no matter what, safety first! People you will come to know and understand, respect, and have pride in their workmanship, who know the true meaning of grit and unwavering support of their coworkers who constantly work closely together, day in and day out. So it's very easy to bond with everyone in the field, and that will straight up tell you...we are our brother's keeper. These are the type of people you will find in this industry.

With that being said, I know for a fact that some individuals avoid opening up to strangers because they are afraid of the reactions that they are going to get. I mean, you can be all friendly and kind and still be treated with disrespect and hostility for no reason. There's always that risk because everything we do is risky. But if we don't dare to do these bold things, we can miss out on a lot of opportunities. You must have the openness to create new relationships and to form new connections as you enter unknown territories and environments.

When you take such a big step into a new industry and you face so many scary, new things, bonding with good people who follow the same path you follow is going to make the experience much more enjoyable. The truth is that the majority of people around us are really good people, and those who are not so good can be easily avoided once you realize who you are dealing with. And when you join a new industry, you are joining a group of people who have similar, if not the same, goals you have, and that is to make good, decent money and to be able to support their families.

## The Right Connection to Open Doors

# Tip #5

Connecting with people around you at a new workplace will also open doors for different job opportunities that could not have been opened otherwise. Every big company's culture is usually developed by the very people who are working for it. Being part of a viable and strong work culture is the engine that will allow you to grow into your fullest professional potential.

My advice for anyone who is entering this industry is to keep an open mind and an open heart to the people you are going to meet in this new workplace. Don't try to form preconceived ideas about the people you are going to meet. Treat every person as a blank page, and let the relationship paint the picture that it will naturally paint. Don't bring past experiences or pains into new relationships, even if those relationships gravitate only around work.

Like I said before, everything we do in life is risky. But if you take this risk and try to bond with those around you in this workplace, you will build strong friendships along the way. These friendships will make the transition to this new extreme much more enjoyable, and they will also help your career grow to heights that you can't imagine.

I became friends with many people while pursuing this new career. I remember the lovely married couple that was in the same OSHA class I was in offering me some of their premade lunch and the outgoing and bubbly OSHA trainer who taught me all there is to know about all of the OSHA 30 standards: the potential hazards and how to work safely in the plant industry. She even taught me how to drive and operate a mini forklift! And then she later died of a horrible disease called lupus, God rest her soul.

Once I completed my training from the school, I went to the Houston area Health and Safety Council (HASC) to test on everything I had learned in her class. I was very grateful to have found the school and that she offered this type of training, because I was able to pass and receive my HASC card in no time! Shortly thereafter I was offered my first gig at a bottling plant!

As I found my way working an oil and gas chemical plant job opportunity, there was this heavy-set older white gentleman, who was very friendly and helpful in helping me remain employed, and he provided me with tips on how to obtain a career in safety (this is the same man I mentioned earlier in this book).

He was a safety manager himself, working for another construction company, and was on the same project I was working on at the time. He further stated that he noticed my good work ethic, and once my initial job assignment ended from the other company I was working for, he immediately had me hired on directly with their company as a paint coating specialist.

I was able to connect with so many different people as I journeyed my way through this industry. And I can't express enough the gratitude I have for the people who helped me along the way; these newfound friendships and bonds I've made during the course of my extreme career change and transition. In return I will try my best to do the same in helping others in need, as I found it necessary to carry on this mindset and tradition, which is the very reason why I wrote this self-help extreme career change book.

My final point is that it's very essential to connect with like-minded people who care and want to see you win and grow, not only as an individual but also in your career goals. Having this type of support right off the bat could be a game changer when it comes to having a smooth and productive transition toward not only a new career but especially one that crosses into an extreme industry. Even if you find that networking and connecting might not help you get where you are trying to go much faster, it definitively makes the experience much more enjoyable.

## Look at the Bright Side

Aside from the hard and grueling plant life work itself, the people are the best part of this job industry. I enjoyed spending time with the crews (the field hands), making friends and laughing at their funny jokes along the way. I enjoyed working on several projects with people from all the other crafts too. I enjoyed the sense of community, camaraderie, and friendship that was developed at the workplace out in the harsh field.

The plant project sites I was fortunate to work on were like meeting up with distant cousins and being with one giant, crazy but fun family; at times it felt like my second home when I was away for extended periods of time. People around you will always be supportive and willing to help you with problems that you might face from time to time, whether at work or in your personal life.

Another positive—or maybe not so positive—I would like to share about working in this industry is that it has its challenges. I love a good challenge and so should you! Challenges make you think outside the box and come up with a better solution. You quickly will adopt the "work smart and not hard" mentality working out in the field along with challenging weather conditions and other seen and unseen elements.

You will learn a lot about time management and how to push yourself outside of your comfort zone. Always remember that when you are surrounded by good, honest, and positive, hard-working people who support you and want you to do your best work, it encourages you to do better, to give it your all, and to continue your career-growth journey no matter what!

The only limits that you are going to experience are the ones you set for yourself. The only true obstacle will be your own mindset. You must first break free of any limitations you set for yourself before changing careers. Especially if you are considering working in the EPC oil and gas plant industry.

I've said it once and I'll say it again: having an end goal is very important in order to keep you focused on the prize. You need to be crystal clear about where you want to go and what you have to do in order to get there. I've already laid out the foundation to start on this path; the rest is up to you! (Refer to my industry study notes page for more information.) This industry provided me much more than financial stability. Working on a new-construction plant refinery project helped me grow beyond my mental and physical expectations, going past distances that I thought were impossible for me as a feminine woman.

Not only did I progress professionally but also personally, thanks to those who influenced me to go for it initially and to my unwavering decision to have faith in God and make that extreme career move. If you would just take advantage of your current or past hardships and tough circumstances, you would be surprised by the things you can achieve and will accomplish in life!

*Remember all the times you won.*
*Practice positive talking and posing.*
*Try to empower others.*

# CHAPTER 9

# SET HIGH STANDARDS AND BE THE CHANGE

*What you do makes a difference, and you have to decide
what kind of difference you want to make.*

—*Jane Goodall*

Standards are the guidelines our mind follows when we take actions and make decisions. They are not mere concepts that don't have any effect on us. Standards are literally life changing. Let me explain how they work. Our mind is like a computer, and any computer needs software to run, just like your laptop needs Windows or Mac OS. The standards you have are the software that includes the blueprint of your life.

Just like the construction workers follow a blueprint when they build something, your mind follows your standards to build your life through guided actions and decisions.

"But what if I don't have any standards?"

In that case, your mind borrows the standards you observe around you. That's why it's best to set standards for yourself. Because you rarely witness good standards from outside sources.

## Tip #6

Set high standards for what kind of person you want to be, what kind of life you want to have, and what you will tolerate or will not tolerate in your life. Having the standard to be a person with unshakable self-confidence is the first and most important step to making it a reality.

And the amount of self-confidence we have in life is proportional to how successful we are and how well we deal with hardships. Self-confidence is the emotional foundation on which we build everything else. If you have a strong foundation, your building is going to last. If not, even a gust of wind can make everything fall apart.

Considering that this industry is tough, self-confidence is even more necessary than in other industries. Not to mention that panicking and being constantly uneasy or nervous can lead to hazardous or deadly mistakes in this case. But how do you build strong self-confidence?

There are five important factors that influence how much you believe in yourself:

1. Setting high standards

2. Forgiving yourself

3. Remembering all the times you won

4.  Practicing positive talking and posture

5.  Trying to empower others

## Remember All the Times You Won

It's easy to focus on the negative side of things and only remember the times we have failed, simply because focusing on something bad is an automatic process in our brain. We are made to quickly notice bad things because that's what keeps us alive as a species.

But in today's world, it is much easier to exaggerate the negative and only see the bad side of things. That means it is much easier to view ourselves as failures, and that is a self-confidence killer. By making a daily habit to *remember all the times you've won* in life, you will train your mind to see the bright side of life, and it will also make you feel better about yourself.

That doesn't mean you won't fail at times, but that doesn't make you a failure either. As I once said, failure is just a stepping stone to success. Remembering how great you are at achieving things will make you feel more confident in your ability to figure things out. And that's all you need to take with you on the road to success.

## Practice Positive Talking and Posture

We are constantly surrounded by negativity. Everywhere you look it's almost a certainty that someone will complain about something or talk down to someone. Add to the fact our brain is wired to focus on bad things as well, and that means we need to make an extra effort to keep ourselves mentally positive.

Controlling all the thoughts you have all the time is an impossible task. What we can control, instead, is the input we feed into our minds. Start with listening to audiobooks and reading books that uplift your spirit and enlighten your mind. Anything from Jim Rohn, Tony Robbins, Brian Tracy, Robin Sharma, Les Brown, or Darren Hardy is a positive food for your brain. By feeding your mind with these positive ideas and visions, it will be much easier to have *positive self-talk* as well.

Now start encouraging yourself on a daily basis and talk about how beautiful, powerful, and amazing you are. You have to be your biggest fan in the world if you want to achieve great things in life. Use the first person when you talk about yourself, like, "I am strong, I am beautiful, I am capable."

And lastly walk like a winner and stand like a winner. Physiology greatly affects our emotional state. That's why no matter who you are, if you stand like you are afraid, sad, or depressed, you are going to feel that way. So walk like Wonder Woman or Superman and feel amazing while doing it. You will be surprised by how good you are going to feel and actually look to others.

There's also a pose that you can practice at home called the power pose, which involves standing like a superhero for three minutes, which will make you feel great.

## Try to Empower Others

Positive and optimistic people lift other people, while negative and pessimistic people try to bring them down. When you encourage and *empower others* by making them feel better about themselves, you will feel better about yourself as well.

Having self-confidence is great, but often it can be selfish when we don't help others out. That's why some people avoid it altogether and call it ego. Ego appears when you think you are the best in the world and no one else. Self-confidence means you think you are the best version of yourself while others can be their best versions as well.

To be a beacon of hope, a ray of light to someone during times of uncertainty, all it takes are small words of praise and encouragement delivered to that person in difficult times. People will appreciate it when you express yourself and mean it from the heart.

You really have to care enough about people around you and treat them like you want to be treated. With that being said, spreading around positivity and having a good perspective on life will be gratifying and fulfilling to you; others will feel uplifted simply being around you as well.

My final food for thought: some people tend to be way too harsh on themselves, and that produces wounds that are hard to heal. If you see yourself as flawed and unworthy, self-confidence takes a major hit. Making mistakes is part of human nature; it is how we grow and learn. Good decisions are made by good experiences and bad experiences are made by bad decisions.

Mistakes don't make us less than others. In fact, the more you fail, the more you can succeed. Failures are simply the building blocks of an amazing life ahead. That's why a master has failed many more times than an apprentice could even try.

So it's time to forgive yourself and acknowledge your greatness. You are awesome and you deserve it all. You also deserve all the love in the world, especially your own. Self-love is not being selfish; it's taking care of your mental and physical state so you can be the best version of yourself possible. And the best part of loving yourself unconditionally is it allows you to build strong self-confidence—no more trying to look perfect and being afraid to make mistakes.

In closing make the effort to do these things daily, and you will soon see the fruits of your labor, which will mean having the ability to tackle your life and the problems that appear with full strength, wisdom, and determination. Because self-confidence will make the best version of yourself come alive.

I hope the six tips shared throughout this book are helpful to you when you must face the difficult side of life. Whether it be making a career change, starting a new business, etc. After all, success is at the other end of adversity, so the better we get at fixing problems, the better we get at achieving great levels of success.

Be confident and remember that you can achieve anything you put your mind to.

*Figure 9: Dee at employer's ribbon-cutting ceremony, photo credit:* www.AlexandersPortraits.com

# CHAPTER 10

# BONUS INDUSTRY STUDY NOTES

## My Closing Remarks

If you have read this book all the way to the end and you're at a pause in the type of career choices you should make to enhance your life and lifestyle for yourself and/or your family, then just know I was once in your shoes. I know how difficult it can be to not have the right information to start on the right track and how it can be extremely stressful, thinking about taking on an extreme career change challenge, mainly into an industry that requires you to pass a test, but not knowing who, what, where, or how to prepare yourself for it. I had to go through this struggle, but you don't have to.

As I promised you, I created special bonus material for readers who purchased my self-help book on extreme career change over to the EPC oil and gas industry (if interested), and it cannot be found anywhere else. These are my personal study notes that touch on various industry terms and meanings that are safety and health-related, particularly working at a new-construction chemical plant or any other type of industrial plant for that matter!

Most of the information captured in my notes can cross various industries because safety and health are the number one goal for most companies, whether it is an office setting, retail, medical, or working at a fast-food or five-star restaurant.

You will also find that my industry study notes are newbie friendly and are written in such a way as to help newbies quickly get familiar with and possibly help you get a better grasp on most of the terms used by the safety council. This will help when you are presented with a series of test questions while trying to obtain a local OSHA card. *(Disclaimer: my study notes do not guarantee that you will pass. They are strictly for informational purposes only.)*

The study notes have a lot of the information you need to kick-start your journey, including a list of companies that took the Workers for America pledge and may offer skilled trade or on-the-job paid training programs. Not only will you receive an exclusive copy of my industry study notes, you will also receive updates whenever I publish new book releases that may inspire, motivate, and/or provide other self-help related stories of interest to you.

For more information on how to obtain the industry study notes email me personally at:

**info@DwanaToldMe.com**

I hope this book helps to further expand your mindset, skills, and income level to their highest potential. See you on the other side!

# Acknowledgments

## Giving Glory to God

First and foremost, I want to thank God almighty for allowing me the free will to endure and overcome the trials and tribulations of one's own life-making decisions, both good and bad. This allowed me to witness and give praise to the miracle He performed in my life by showing me His mercy and, giving me the ability to become more aware of making better judgements and to tap further into my life's purpose.

## To the Ones Who Kick-Started My Journey

Writing a book is a lot harder than I thought yet more rewarding than I could have ever imagined. But none of this would have been possible had it not been for my stepbrother, Andre. He was the first I reached out to, seeking his help in trying to enter the oil and gas industry, only because he was already working at the chemical plants. He took me under his wing and helped point me to the first sign of hope! And for that I'm eternally grateful. I also want to give a big thank you to Missy, my first OSHA safety instructor (may she rest in peace). Her home-like school and teaching style helped me pass the safety council tests with flying colors. And then there was Timesha, a true "go-getter" helped me land my first plant gig at a bottling plant and then off to the races I went, and I have never looked back since!

## To Family and Close Friends

I want to thank my mom, Brenda, for staying in my corner and making sure I don't forget to mention her in my book! My sister Mya, my cousin Chabli, and my good friends Shante, Wanda "Twinsie," and Martin Jamal, for attempting to help me with the initial dreaded edits and critiquing on the first rough draft of this book. I also thank my aunt Mary and my friend Mariah for patiently helping me pick and choose the subtitle to my book. And I want to thank everyone else who ever said anything positive to me while I was taking this career-change journey. I heard it all, and it meant a lot to me.

## To All My Former Field Coworkers

I want to thank those (pipefitters, welders, electricians, iron workers, crane & riggers, and millwrights / boilermakers) who have gifted me with your "know, like, and trust" to work alongside you in situations that could cause either of us harm or imminent danger. We have ventured into many new construction projects together, but we have continued to enhance each other with patience, perception, and perseverance. And a special thanks to Pablo and Martin, my former mentors and Felix the awesome on-site Pipefitter program trainer.

## To More Important Colleagues

A "Special Thanks" to Mr. Slaughter, Brook, Brad, Gordon, Mike and all the others who took the time to help me on my career-change journey from point of entry, into the skilled trades Women in Construction program, to the trips made to the White House to help pass the Worker's for America bill. A big thank you to Jason and Kyle for suggesting me in the first place, thus enabling my first trip to the White House. And I want to thank Jim for being a good friend and who's had my best interests at heart at the plant. And finally...

## To You

I thank you who wish to better yourselves by taking the time to read this book. You humble me and encourage me to continue to try to make the world a better place through collaboration!

I feel blessed to have been given the chance to connect or stay connected with many people through my work, coaching, or through life in general.

Thank you all!

# Note From The Author

As I conclude this journey through the realms of professional growth and personal development, I am compelled to reflect on a fundamental truth: the essence of true success lies not merely in accolades or titles, but in the rich tapestry of one's work history and the depth of their acquired knowledge, interwoven with the myriad experiences of their past.

In our pursuit of excellence within our respective careers, it's easy to become fixated on the tangible markers of success – promotions, salary increments, or recognition. Yet, beneath these external trappings lies a more profound measure of achievement: the wealth of wisdom garnered through years of dedication, perseverance, and the invaluable lessons learned from both triumphs and setbacks.

Indeed, it is the amalgamation of professional expertise and the mosaic of life experiences that truly distinguishes an individual's journey towards fulfillment and accomplishment. Each challenge surmounted, every obstacle overcome, contributes to the shaping of not only a proficient professional but also a well-rounded individual capable of navigating the complexities of both career and life with resilience and grace.

As we embark on new endeavors and chart the course of our futures, let us remember that true success is not a destination but rather a continuous odyssey of growth and self-discovery. May we cherish the richness of our work history and the depth of our knowledge, recognizing that it is through the integration of these elements that we forge the path to enduring fulfillment and true prosperity in both our professional endeavors and our lives as a whole.

Let's talk! Connect with me at:

www.DwanaToldMe.com

www.ingramcontent.com/pod-product-compliance
Lightning Source LLC
Chambersburg PA
CBHW062113080426
42734CB00012B/2850